PRACTICE

CULTURAL CURRICULUM

Name: _____ Class: _____

Table of Contents

Introduction ⸻ 2

NY-1.OA.1 ⸻ 3

Use addition and subtraction within 20 to solve one step word problems involving situations of adding to, taking from, putting together, taking apart, and/or comparing, with unknowns in all positions.

NY-1.OA.6a. ⸻ 12

Add and subtract within 20. Use strategies such as: counting on; making a ten; decomposing a number leading to a ten; using the relationship between addition and subtraction; and creating equivalent but easier or known sums.

NY-1.NBT.2 ⸻ 21

Understand that the two digits of a two-digit number represent amounts of tens and ones.

NY-1.MD.2 ⸻ 39

Measure the length of an object using same-size "length units" placed end to end with no gaps or overlaps. Express the length of an object as a whole number of "length units."

Proficiency Check 1 ⸻ 48

Proficiency Check 2 ⸻ 59

About Us ⸻ 70

PRACTICE
CULTURAL CURRICULUM

Introduction

First graders, ready to ace your big test? This workbook will help you study smart! We found the most important math problems to know and included QR codes for extra help. Plus, the problems are all about real-life things that you'll use in the future. Let's dominate that test!

Grade 1 Topics:

1. **Operations and Algebraic Thinking**
   a. Represent and solve problems involving addition and subtraction.
   b. Add and subtract within 20.
2. **Numbers and Operations in Base Ten**
   a. Understand place value.
3. **Measurement and Data**
   a. Measure lengths indirectly and by iterating length units.

Grade 1 High Priority New York State Math Standards:

1. NY-1.OA.1 Use addition and subtraction within 20 to solve one step word problems involving situations of adding to, taking from, putting together, taking apart, and/or comparing, with unknowns in all positions.

2. NY-1.OA.6a. Add and subtract within 20. Use strategies such as: counting on; making a ten; decomposing a number leading to a ten; using the relationship between addition and subtraction; and creating equivalent but easier or known sums.

3. NY-1.NBT.2 Understand that the two digits of a two-digit number represent amounts of tens and ones.

4. NY-1.MD.2 Measure the length of an object using same-size "length units" placed end to end with no gaps or overlaps. Express the length of an object as a whole number of "length units."

NY-1.OA.1 Use addition and subtraction within 20 to solve one step word problems involving situations of adding to, taking from, putting together, taking apart, and/or comparing, with unknowns in all positions.

Watch: Count on from one embedded number or part to totals of 6 and 7, and generate all addition expressions for each total.

(Represent and solve problems involving addition and subtraction. Add and subtract within 20.)

Link: https://youtu.be/ZGyUpheFo-c

NY-1.OA.1 Use addition and subtraction within 20 to solve one step word problems involving situations of adding to, taking from, putting together, taking apart, and/or comparing, with unknowns in all positions.

Independent practice question:

There are 5 foxes. One fox joins them. How many foxes are there in all? Draw a picture and write a number sentence to show your thinking.

NY-1.OA.1 Use addition and subtraction within 20 to solve one step word problems involving situations of adding to, taking from, putting together, taking apart, and/or comparing, with unknowns in all positions.

Independent practice question:

There are 2 turtles in the garden. Then, 5 turtles join them. How many turtles are there in all? Draw a picture and write a number sentence to show your thinking.

NY-1.OA.1 Use addition and subtraction within 20 to solve one step word problems involving situations of adding to, taking from, putting together, taking apart, and/or comparing, with unknowns in all positions.

Watch: Represent all the number pairs of 10 as number bonds from a given scenario, and generate all expressions equal to 10.

(Represent and solve problems involving addition and subtraction. Add and subtract within 20.)

Link: https://youtu.be/d1FBz_Rpk90

NY-1.OA.1 Use addition and subtraction within 20 to solve one step word problems involving situations of adding to, taking from, putting together, taking apart, and/or comparing, with unknowns in all positions.

Independent practice question:

Fill in the ten frame. Write an equation that will represent completing the ten frame.

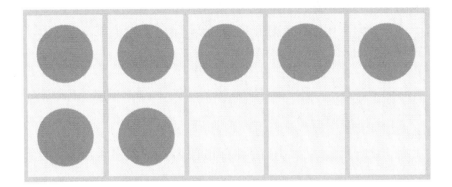

NY-1.OA.1 Use addition and subtraction within 20 to solve one step word problems involving situations of adding to, taking from, putting together, taking apart, and/or comparing, with unknowns in all positions.

Independent practice question:

Fill in the ten frame. Write an equation that will represent completing the ten frame.

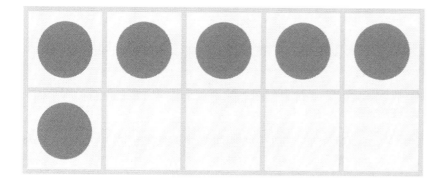

NY-1.OA.1 Use addition and subtraction within 20 to solve one step word problems involving situations of adding to, taking from, putting together, taking apart, and/or comparing, with unknowns in all positions.

Watch: <u>Count on from one embedded number or part to totals of 6 and 7, and generate all addition expressions for each total.</u>

(Represent and solve problems involving addition and subtraction. Add and subtract within 20.)

Link: https://youtu.be/Ad2z2ARBaHA

NY-1.OA.1 Use addition and subtraction within 20 to solve one step word problems involving situations of adding to, taking from, putting together, taking apart, and/or comparing, with unknowns in all positions.

Independent practice question:

Mrs. Wong's class raised two groups of silkworms. In one group, 3 silkworms turned into moths. In the other group, 4 silkworms turned into a moth. In total, how many silkworms turned into moths? Write an addition sentence that fits the story.

NY-1.OA.1 Use addition and subtraction within 20 to solve one step word problems involving situations of adding to, taking from, putting together, taking apart, and/or comparing, with unknowns in all positions.

Independent practice question:

Belle only feeds her dog two kinds of treats. Last month, Belle fed her dog 5 peanut butter treats and 2 carrot treats. How many dog treats did Belle feed her dog last month? Write an addition sentence that fits the story.

NY-1.OA.6a. Add and subtract within 20. Use strategies such as: counting on; making a ten; decomposing a number leading to a ten; using the relationship between addition and subtraction; and creating equivalent but easier or known sums.

Watch: <u>Count on from one embedded number or part to totals of 8 and 9, and generate all expressions for each total.</u>

(Represent and solve problems involving addition and subtraction. Add and subtract within 20.)

Link: <u>https://youtu.be/nkFfhOzlauE</u>

NY-1.OA.6a. Add and subtract within 20. Use strategies such as: counting on; making a ten; decomposing a number leading to a ten; using the relationship between addition and subtraction; and creating equivalent but easier or known sums.

Independent practice question:

Ms. Fitz has 4 binders on her bookshelf. One of her students donated 4 binders. How many binders are there in all? Draw a picture and write a number sentence to show your thinking.

NY-1.OA.6a. Add and subtract within 20. Use strategies such as: counting on; making a ten; decomposing a number leading to a ten; using the relationship between addition and subtraction; and creating equivalent but easier or known sums.

Independent practice question:

During a hot weekend, Shai eats 3 cherry popsicles and 6 strawberry popsicles. How many popsicles did he eat in all? Draw a picture and write a number sentence to show your thinking.

NY-1.OA.6a. Add and subtract within 20. Use strategies such as: counting on; making a ten; decomposing a number leading to a ten; using the relationship between addition and subtraction; and creating equivalent but easier or known sums.

Watch: Addition math stories by drawing, writing equations, and making statements of the solution.

(Represent and solve problems involving addition and subtraction. Add and subtract within 20.)

Link: https://youtu.be/2QsDB6vRwo8

NY-1.OA.6a. Add and subtract within 20. Use strategies such as: counting on; making a ten; decomposing a number leading to a ten; using the relationship between addition and subtraction; and creating equivalent but easier or known sums.

Independent practice question:

There are 15 tadpoles in a pond. 5 tadpoles swim up to join the group. How many tadpoles are there in all? Draw a picture and write a number sentence to show your thinking.

NY-1.OA.6a. Add and subtract within 20. Use strategies such as: counting on; making a ten; decomposing a number leading to a ten; using the relationship between addition and subtraction; and creating equivalent but easier or known sums.

Independent practice question:

Draw a number bond for the following number sentence. 12 + 6 = 18

NY-1.OA.6a. Add and subtract within 20. Use strategies such as: counting on; making a ten; decomposing a number leading to a ten; using the relationship between addition and subtraction; and creating equivalent but easier or known sums.

Watch: Represent all the number pairs of 10 as number bonds from a given scenario, and generate all expressions equal to 10.

(Represent and solve problems involving addition and subtraction. Add and subtract within 20.)

Link: https://youtu.be/W_oYW05pFeU

NY-1.OA.6a. Add and subtract within 20. Use strategies such as: counting on; making a ten; decomposing a number leading to a ten; using the relationship between addition and subtraction; and creating equivalent but easier or known sums.

Independent practice question:

Melody has 5 pink shirts and 3 blue bottoms. Kairah has 4 yellow shorts and 4 black bottoms. Who has more pieces of clothing?

NY-1.OA.6a. Add and subtract within 20. Use strategies such as: counting on; making a ten; decomposing a number leading to a ten; using the relationship between addition and subtraction; and creating equivalent but easier or known sums.

Independent practice question:

Jane bought 2 pairs of earrings and 9 beaded bracelets. Jolie bought 4 pairs of earrings and 8 beaded bracelets. Who has more jewelry?

NY-1.MD.2 Measure the length of an object using same-size "length units" placed end to end with no gaps or overlaps. Express the length of an object as a whole number of "length units."

Watch: <u>Order, measure, and compare the length of objects before and after measuring with centimeter cubes, solving with differences unknown word problems.</u>

(Measure lengths indirectly and by iterating length units.)

Link: <u>https://youtu.be/FwJMl3qTARU</u>

PRACTICE
CULTURAL CURRICULUM

NY-1.MD.2 Measure the length of an object using same-size "length units" placed end to end with no gaps or overlaps. Express the length of an object as a whole number of "length units."

Independent practice question:

At the Doggie Boutique, the t-shirts are 16 cm long. The sweatshirts are 3 cm longer than the t-shirts. How long are the sweatshirts?

NY-1.MD.2 Measure the length of an object using same-size "length units" placed end to end with no gaps or overlaps. Express the length of an object as a whole number of "length units."

Independent practice question:

At Sophie's Candy Shop, the cherry lollipops are 10 cm long. The butterscotch sticks are 2 cm longer than the cherry lollipops. The chocolate bars are 4 cm shorter than the cherry lollipops. How long are the butterscotch sticks?

NY-1.MD.2 Measure the length of an object using same-size "length units" placed end to end with no gaps or overlaps. Express the length of an object as a whole number of "length units."

Watch: Express the length of an object using centimeter cubes as length units to measure with no gaps or overlaps.

(Measure lengths indirectly and by iterating length units.)

Link: https://youtu.be/rmP9mpHjZGk

NY-1.MD.2 Measure the length of an object using same-size "length units" placed end to end with no gaps or overlaps. Express the length of an object as a whole number of "length units."

Independent practice question:

Measure the following images using a centimeter ruler or centimeter cubes.

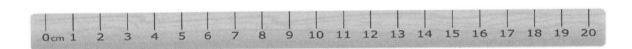

NY-1.MD.2 Measure the length of an object using same-size "length units" placed end to end with no gaps or overlaps. Express the length of an object as a whole number of "length units."

Independent practice question:

Measure the following images using a centimeter ruler or centimeter cubes.

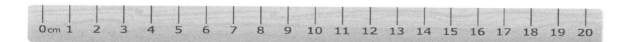

NY-1.MD.2 Measure the length of an object using same-size "length units" placed end to end with no gaps or overlaps. Express the length of an object as a whole number of "length units."

Watch: <u>Rename and measure with centimeter cubes, using their standard unit name of centimeters.</u>

(Measure lengths indirectly and by iterating length units.)

Link: <u>https://youtu.be/NNbXKuZ_IF4</u>

NY-1.MD.2 Measure the length of an object using same-size "length units" placed end to end with no gaps or overlaps. Express the length of an object as a whole number of "length units."

Independent practice question:

How long is the paintbrush in centimeters?
inches?

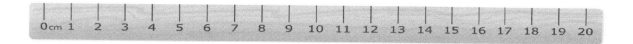

NY-1.MD.2 Measure the length of an object using same-size "length units" placed end to end with no gaps or overlaps. Express the length of an object as a whole number of "length units."

Independent practice question:

How long is this pen in centimeters? Inches?

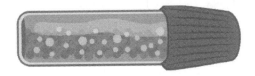

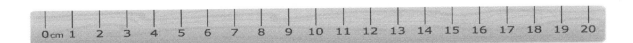

NY-1.MD.2 Measure the length of an object using same-size "length units" placed end to end with no gaps or overlaps. Express the length of an object as a whole number of "length units."

Watch: Measure the same objects with different non-standard units simultaneously to see the need to measure with a consistent unit.

(Measure lengths indirectly and by iterating length units.)

Link: https://youtu.be/0qlAihdi_IM

NY-1.MD.2 Measure the length of an object using same-size "length units" placed end to end with no gaps or overlaps. Express the length of an object as a whole number of "length units."

Independent practice question:

At Red Lobster, knives are 13 centimeters long. Spoons are 4 centimeters longer than knives. How many centimeters long are the spoons at Red Lobster? Show your thinking.

NY-1.MD.2 Measure the length of an object using same-size "length units" placed end to end with no gaps or overlaps. Express the length of an object as a whole number of "length units."

Independent practice question:

Romee plays with his bath boost toys. His yellow boat is 7 centimeters long. His red boat is 1 centimeter shorter than the yellow boat. How long is the red boat? Show your thinking.

NY-1.MD.2 Measure the length of an object using same-size "length units" placed end to end with no gaps or overlaps. Express the length of an object as a whole number of "length units."

Watch: <u>Answer compare with difference unknown problems about lengths of two different objects measured in centimeters.</u>

(Measure lengths indirectly and by iterating length units.)

Link: <u>https://youtu.be/3fUO9xiGP0A</u>

NY-1.MD.2 Measure the length of an object using same-size "length units" placed end to end with no gaps or overlaps. Express the length of an object as a whole number of "length units."

Independent practice question:

Using centimeter cubes or an online centimeter ruler...

How much longer is the top flashlight from the bottom flashlight?

NY-1.MD.2 Measure the length of an object using same-size "length units" placed end to end with no gaps or overlaps. Express the length of an object as a whole number of "length units."

Independent practice question:

Using centimeter cubes or an online centimeter ruler…

How much longer is the pencil at the top from the bottom pencil?

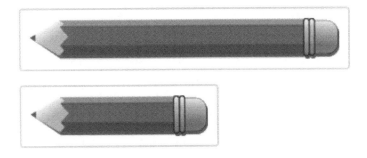

NY-1.MD.2 Measure the length of an object using same-size "length units" placed end to end with no gaps or overlaps. Express the length of an object as a whole number of "length units."

Watch: Understand the need to use the same units when comparing measurements with others.

(Measure lengths indirectly and by iterating length units.)

Link: https://youtu.be/JwmiQrhV9CA

NY-1.MD.2 Measure the length of an object using same-size "length units" placed end to end with no gaps or overlaps. Express the length of an object as a whole number of "length units."

Independent practice question:

Devon and Max are at the beach. Devon's shovel is 5 centimeters long. Max's shovel is 3 centimeters long. If they use their shovel to measure the length of their 15 centimeter beach towel,

    a. How many shovels would Devon use?
    b. How many shovels would Max use?

NY-1.MD.2 Measure the length of an object using same-size "length units" placed end to end with no gaps or overlaps. Express the length of an object as a whole number of "length units."

Independent practice question:

Lemuel and Levi are at school. Lemuel's eraser is 2 centimeters long. Levi's eraser is 4 centimeters long. If they use their eraser to measure the length of their 8 centimeter pencil,

    a. How many erasers would Lemuel use?
    b. How many erasers would Levi use?

NY-1.NBT.2 Understand that the two digits of a two-digit number represent amounts of tens and ones.

Watch: Solve addition and subtraction problems decomposing and composing teen numbers as 1 ten and some ones

(Understand place value.)

Link: https://youtu.be/mglry85fml8

NY-1.NBT.2 Understand that the two digits of a two-digit number represent amounts of tens and ones.

Independent practice question:

What number is shown below? Solve: 19 - 7 = ?

NY-1.NBT.2 Understand that the two digits of a two-digit number represent amounts of tens and ones.

Independent practice question::

What number is shown below? Solve: 18 - 9 = ?

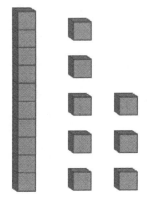

NY-1.NBT.2 Understand that the two digits of a two-digit number represent amounts of tens and ones.

Watch: Solve addition problems using ten as a unit, and write two-step solutions.

(Understand place value.)

Link: https://youtu.be/cHxFNVoghOM

NY-1.NBT.2 Understand that the two digits of a two-digit number represent amounts of tens and ones.

Independent practice question:

If 9 + 4 = 13, create a drawing and number bond of the sum of 13 using a group of ten.

NY-1.NBT.2 Understand that the two digits of a two-digit number represent amounts of tens and ones.

Independent practice question:

If 7 + 7 = 14, create a drawing and number bond of the sum of 14 using a group of ten.

NY-1.NBT.2 Understand that the two digits of a two-digit number represent amounts of tens and ones.

Watch: <u>Solve subtraction problems using ten as a unit, and write two-step solutions.</u>

(Understand place value.)

Link: <u>https://youtu.be/qyIzk9hXDyU</u>

NY-1.NBT.2 Understand that the two digits of a two-digit number represent amounts of tens and ones.

Independent practice question:

There are 120 students who eat school lunch.

A mama bear and her cub caught a total of 21 fish. Her cub caught 15 fish. How many fish did the mama bear catch?

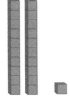

NY-1.NBT.2 Understand that the two digits of a two-digit number represent amounts of tens and ones.

Independent practice question:

Tom's cats caught a total of 14 mice and birds. His cats caught 4 mice. How many birds did Tom's cats catch last year?

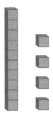

Proficiency Check 1

Hi Scholar! We are thrilled that you have worked so hard in this workbook!

The following questions are used to show your knowledge of the math

topics taught. We wish you the best as you continue to learn and grow!

Directions:

1. Answer each question to the best of your ability.
2. Use the additional space on the page to show your work.
3. Choose your answer by circling the letter or image.
4. Proceed to the next page.
5. Stop at **page 58.**

1. How do you make 10?

A. 3 + 2

B. 5 + 1

C. 3 + 4

D. 2 + 8

2. Fill in the missing number:

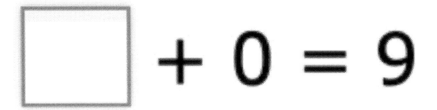

$$\square + 0 = 9$$

A. 2

B. 0

C. 9

D. 1

3. LeCarter just used his allowance to buy some toy dinosaurs. He paid $3, and now he has $1 left. How much money did LeCarter have before buying the toy cars? Choose the addition sentences that fit the story.

A. 1 + 3 = 4

B. 3 + 1 = 4

C. 4 + 1 = 5

D. 3 + 4 = 7

4. Jolie bought 10 gallons of pink paint to paint her room. When she was finished, she had 2 gallons left of unused paint. How many gallons of paint did Jenny use?

A. 12

B. 8

C. 2

D. 0

5. What number is shown?

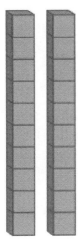

A. 20

B. 10

C. 12

D. 2

6. What number is shown?

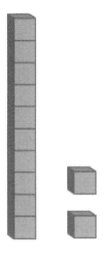

A. 22

B. 12

C. 21

D. 13

7. Choose the missing number.

1 ten + 7 ones =

A. 1

B. 17

C. 71

D. 7

8.Which hammer is the shortest?

○ Hammer #1

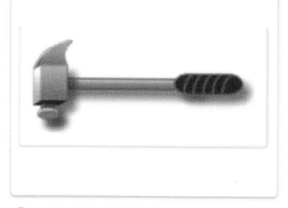

○ Hammer #2

○ Hammer #3

A. Hammer #1

B. Hammer #2

C. Hammer #3

D. They are all the same length

9. Which pen is longer?

◯ Pen #1

◯ Pen #2

A. Pen #1

B. Pen #2

C. They are both the same length

10. Using the ruler as reference, how many inches long is the green bean?

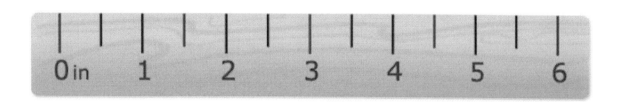

A. 4 inches

B. 6 inches

C. 3 inches

D. 1 inch

Proficiency Check 2

Hi Scholar! We are thrilled that you have worked so hard in this workbook!

The following questions are used to show your knowledge of the math

topics taught. We wish you the best as you continue to learn and grow!

Directions:
1. Answer each question to the best of your ability.
2. Use the additional space on the page to show your work.
3. Choose your answer by circling the letter or image.
4. Proceed to the next page.
5. Stop at **page 69**.

1. Choose the correct addition sentence for this model?

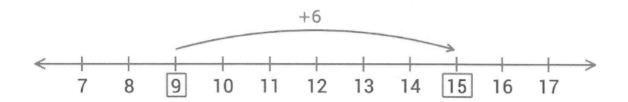

A. 9 + 0 = 9

B. 9 + 6 = 15

C. 6 + 15 = 21

D. 9 + 15 = 24

2. Add:

A. 12

B. 8

C. 17

D. 9

3. Choose the subtraction sentence for this model.

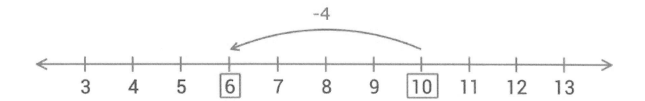

A. 10 - 4 = 6

B. 10 + 4 = 14

C. 6 + 4 = 10

D. 6 - 4 = 2

4. The music school in Brownsville held a children's concert and an adult's concert at the same time. A total of 17 students performed at the two concerts. If 8 students performed at the children's concert, how many students performed at the adult's concert?

A. 17 students

B. 7 students

C. 9 students

D. 25 students

5. Which place value model shows the number: 17?

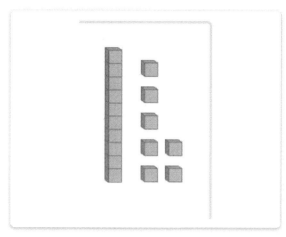

◯ #1

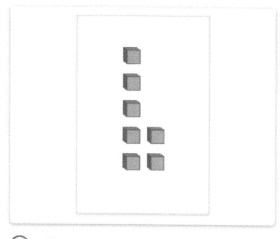

◯ #2

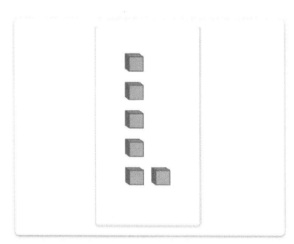

◯ #3

A. #1

B. #2

C. #3

D. #1 & #3

6. What number is shown?

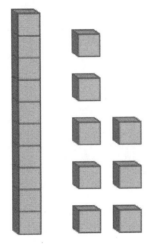

A. 22

B. 18

C. 21

D. 13

7. Which screw driver is longer?

◯ #1

◯ #2

A. #1

B. #2

C. They are the same length

8.Which flower is taller?

○ #1

○ #2

A. #1

B. #2

C. Neither

9. Use the ruler as reference to estimate the length of the twig. How many inches long is the twig?

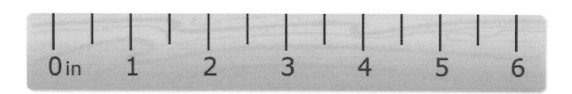

A. 2 inches

B. 3 inches

C. 4 inches

D. 5 inches

10. Cali's straw is 10 inches long. Timothy's straw is 2 inches shorter than Amy's.How long is Timothy's straw?

A. 12 inches

B. 6 inches

C. 3 inches

D. 8 inches

ABOUT US

PRACTICE is a mission-driven business that believes in the power of public schools to build the next generation of urban-educated leaders. We are a New York City-based B-Corp that partners with principals, teachers and parents to close the opportunity gap in urban schools. Our work includes: a rigorous, culturally responsive curricula taught by Education Champions that look like the kids they serve, customized private tutoring solutions for one-on-one learning taught by our most accomplished Education Champions, and software solutions, built to help students succeed, that connect parents and educators and provide real-time insights and data from both inside and outside of the classroom.

VISION

No child's circumstance limits their potential.

MISSION

Advance equitable education for urban students to close the opportunity gap.

CORE VALUES

We have always been a mission driven organization and have had the same core values at PRACTICE since we started over a decade ago. We work incredibly hard to live our values at all levels of the company.

- Excellence - We expect nothing less from the students we serve

- Entrepreneurship – We recognize that innovation and execution are fundamental to improving educational outcomes

- Conscious Capitalism – We are focused on the triple bottom line: people (drivers of change), community (paying it forward), and profit (financial sustainability)

- Revolutionary Change - We seek to be the catalysts that positively disrupt the education status quo

BRAND PROMISES

We have always been a mission driven organization and have had the same core values at PRACTICE since we started over a decade ago. We work incredibly hard to live our values at all levels of the company.

- Programmatic Outcomes – We work relentlessly to meet the individual needs of our students to ensure progress is made towards achieving proficiency

- Professionalism – We hold ourselves to the highest standards from top to bottom

- Full Service Partnership – We do whatever it takes to deliver high quality products and services for our partners

FOUNDER + ORIGIN STORY

Founder and CEO Karim Abouelnaga started PRACTICE while in his dorm room at Cornell University. Karim was raised by a single mother on government aid in New York City where he attended some of the city's most struggling public schools. Thanks to a series of nonprofits and mentors, Karim became the first one in his family to attend college, graduating in the top 10% of his class.

In his first semester at Cornell, he realized the significant difference in his K-12 experience compared to that of many of his friends on campus. There, he rallied a group of classmates to create an organization to level the playing field for low-income children. Karim was determined to change the inequities he experienced in the public schools he grew up in to ensure that a student's zip code doesn't determine their future.

As CEO, Karim understands the importance of first-hand experience when working with urban schools and that is the foundation of our inside-out approach to education. Many of our leadership team and tutors are of and from the communities we serve. A majority of our tutors are college students working on undergraduate or graduate degrees who intimately understand the realities of urban classrooms and are driven to help urban students like themselves reach their full potential.

Have suggestions to make this workbook better? Visit our website www.practicebc.com and Contact Us with your feedback. We look forward to hearing from you!

Made in the USA
Columbia, SC
21 February 2023

12726123R00041